Bison for Kids

by Todd Wilkinson
photography by Michael H. Francis
illustrated by John F. McGee

NorthWord
PRESS, INC
Minocqua, Wisconsin

DEDICATION

For Matthew and Jenna, my brother's children.
— Todd Wilkinson

For Elizabeth Rose and Emily Louise,
my ever inquisitive daughters.
—Michael H. Francis

Copyright ©1994 by Todd Wilkinson
NorthWord Press, Inc.
P.O. Box 1360
Minocqua, WI 54548

Designed by Russell S. Kuepper

For a free catalog describing NorthWord's line of nature books and gifts, call 1-800-336-5666.

ISBN# 1-55971-431-X

Printed in Malaysia

Bison for Kids

by Todd Wilkinson
photography by Michael H. Francis
illustrated by John F. McGee

Quick! Put your ear to the ground and listen. Do you hear the rumble? It comes from some far-off place on the prairie. As the noise gets louder and louder, the ground shakes.

It's not an earthquake.

It's not a thunderstorm.

It's not a train rolling down the tracks.

It's not even your growling stomach.

What could it be?

It's a bunch of bison. That's what. A herd of them causes the ground to shake. Ten thousand hooves kick up a cloud of dust. Where are all these animals going in such a hurry?

To bison country. Let's go along!

Getting there requires a map of the Great Plains. Like a nature detective, finding bison country means searching for clues.

Where bison gather, there are few trees to climb. But grass can grow head high, towering above prairie dogs, and sheep, and owls that build their nests in the ground. Sometimes, there are slithering rattlesnakes and coyotes and foxes, too. Many different animals live near bison. And stubby little shrubs called sagebrush grow at their feet. A great clue and one of the best things to look for is cowbirds, because cowbirds perch on top of bison heads to inspect the countryside. It takes a lot of nerve to sit on a bison's head!

Although bison look familiar, most people know them by another name: American b-u-f-f-a-l-o. Bison were given this nickname by French explorers who took one look at the husky, four-legged grass-eaters and said: "Les boeufs," which is French for "the beef." They thought bison were wild cows or oxen.

The French explorers were partially right. Bison have horns, hooves, and teeth just like cows and oxen. They *are* related—as all members of the bovine family—but they're not the same beasts.

Bison also have close ties with people. For thousands of years, bison and Native Americans lived side by side and shared the prairie. Many tribes still consider bison to be their brothers. They believe that long ago when the world was formed, bison could turn themselves into humans, and humans could become bison. In fact, the Sioux Indians have their own special name for bison, "Tatanka" (TAH-TONG-KUH). But no matter what we humans call bison, seeing one is amazing. It makes hearts beat fast because bison are huge and they really *do* weigh a ton.

Now, bison roam free in only a few places, but they are popular animals. Maybe you know the words to the pioneer song, *Home On The Range*:

Oh Give Me A Home
Where The Buffalo Roam
Where The Deer And The Antelope Play
Where Seldom Is Heard
A Discouraging Word
And The Skies Are Not Cloudy All Day
Home, Home On the Range

People remember bison in more than songs. Some cities are named after buffalo. The animals are the mascots for football teams and the symbols of important branches of the government, like the U.S. Department of Interior. Bison even had their pictures engraved on a coin. In 1913, the U.S. government made a "buffalo nickel" with the picture of a bison on one side and the face of an Indian on the other. The government stopped making buffalo nickels in 1938, so they are very rare today, like the wild bison. Most bison live in parks, zoos, and private ranches between the Mississippi River and the Rocky Mountains. The rarest bison of all is the white buffalo, which is worshipped by Native Americans. One white buffalo named "Big Medicine" has been mounted by a taxidermist and put on display at the Montana Historical Society in Helena, Montana.

Each year, millions of people drive to Yellowstone National Park in Wyoming to see the world's most famous bison herds. In Yellowstone, you might see a bison on your way to the Old Faithful Geyser or spot one standing next to a grizzly bear or in big open valleys. Besides Yellowstone, there are almost a dozen different places where people can see bison.

At one time—maybe 400 years ago—60 million bison (that's a 6 with seven zeroes behind it), were alive on the prairies of North America. With so many bison, parts of the Great Plains must have looked like a giant, jumbled piece of chocolate cake.

The first bison came to North America one million years ago when they made the long journey from Asia. Even before Indian tribes traveled to North America, huge ancestors of the modern bison, known as the wisent (VEE-SENT), roamed far and wide. The wisent, which also lived in Europe, crossed a narrow strip of land that connected Russia to Alaska. From Alaska, thousands of wisent moved south into what is now the lower United States and Canada.

Scientists who dig up bison fossils know this because

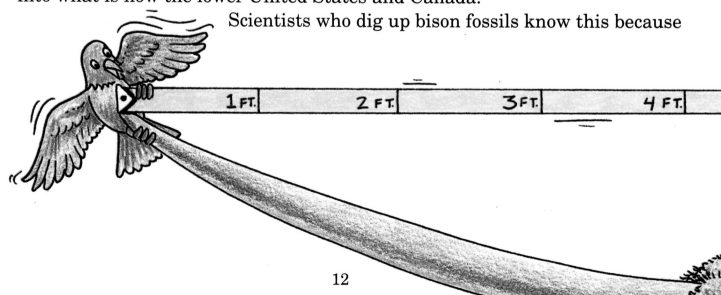

12

they have found wisent skulls with horns nine feet across.

In all the world, only three different kinds of bison remain. They are smaller than the ancient wisent. The wood bison lives mostly in the forests and meadows of western Canada, the plains bison roams across the heart of the United States, and the European wisent exists today mostly in zoos and preserves. Bison are great survivors. While other big animals—woolly mammoths, prehistoric horses and camels—died out and became extinct from changing weather and human hunters, wood and plains bison managed to stay alive. They were in bison country during the Ice Age when glaciers covered much of the United States and Canada. When the ice melted, bison spread out in search of green grass. And Native American tribes followed the mighty herds.

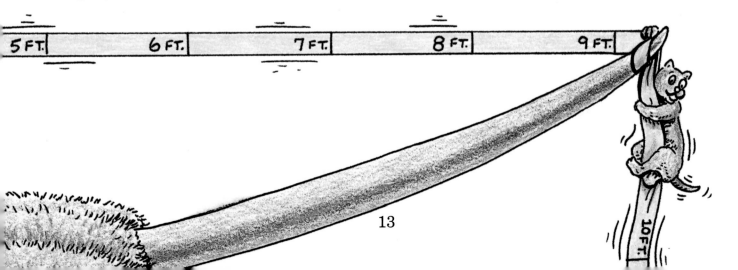

5 FT. | 6 FT. | 7 FT. | 8 FT. | 9 FT. | 10 FT.

Thousands of years ago, human artists made drawings of bison across cave walls in the northern half of the world. Those pictures are called pictographs and petroglyphs. The oldest drawing of a bison in North America

was published in a book 60 years after Columbus sailed to the New World. Back then, bison seemed to be everywhere. When Daniel Boone and other pioneers started to explore the American wilderness, they found bison as far east as Kentucky.

What happened after that is a sad story. Hunters killed millions of buffalo for food and hides. Settlers slaughtered them to make room on the Great Plains for cattle. One of the most famous bison hunters was William "Buffalo Bill" Cody, who delivered mail for the Pony Express and shot bison to feed railroad workers. He killed thousands of bison. As a result of the overhunting, only a few hundred wild buffalo were left in the United States at the end of the 1800s.

Bison needed to be protected fast! Otherwise they were doomed to disappear from the world forever. After Congress created Yellowstone as the world's first national park in 1872, bison were brought there to live in safety. And today there are 3,000 in the park.

What makes a bison special to see? The first thing you notice is its size. The bison is the biggest mammal to inhabit North America. A full-grown bison weighs about 2,000 pounds (more than some cars!). It can also sprint as fast as a horse—up to 35 miles per hour—and stand as tall as a professional football player. Male bison, known as "bulls," can grow twice as big as female bison, called "cows."

A bison has shapes as no other animal. It has a hump on its back that looks like a camel's. Some people think the hump holds water, but it doesn't. The hump is really a large shoulder muscle that holds up the bison's huge, shaggy head. A bison also has a dark mop-top pile of hair on its head and a thick, brown beard attached to its chin. It has patches of fur that flare out on its legs called pantaloons and hair tufts on the end of its tail. It may look soft, but the fur on a bison is rough; it feels like wool on a sheep.

Above a bison's eyes are curved horns that protrude from the skull on both bulls and cows, sometimes stretching three feet from tip to tip.

Some people think bison are mean looking and ornery. Others think they are peaceful and slow. But after they learn more about how bison live, they sometimes change their minds.

Bison are social animals. They gather in crowds, just like people. When they travel, bison walk together in herds across the hills and valleys.

By staying close to their mothers' sides, baby bison feel safe from predators such as wolves, coyotes, mountain lions, bears, and people.

Spring in bison country is a special time. As flowers bloom, bison mothers give birth to one small, reddish calf. Baby bison have wobbly legs but soon learn to walk and suckle milk from their mothers' bellies. Within a few months after they are born, bison calves begin sprouting horns that stay on their heads and grow the rest of their lives. And the hump on their back begins to broaden, too.

By a calf's first birthday, it weighs between three and four hundred pounds—as much as a sofa and about ten times more than it weighed at birth. A calf leaves its mother after its second birthday, when it is considered a young adult. But it takes a bison another six years before it is full grown and ready to start a family of its own.

While cows nurse their calves, bulls stray away from the herd and go off by themselves. They do little to help raise their offspring. Bulls return to the herd in July and August to tangle with other bulls and to gain the attention of cows. This clashing of bulls is known as "the rut." During the rut, two bulls line up several feet away from each other then charge forward and wrestle head to head, horn to horn. It causes quite a commotion. The jousting may last minutes or it may be over in seconds. After a dominant bull wins these matches, other males respect and fear him. He has earned the right to mate with a female.

A little over nine months later (about the same time it takes a human baby to develop), the cow lays down on her side and gives birth to the new calf. The mother gives her young a welcome to the world by gently licking birth fluids from her baby's shiny coat. After two months, the baby's red fur starts turning brown.

Adult bison live for about 12 years, but scientists have found some real old-timers that have reached their 40th birthday. During the winter when the snow gets deep, bison use their heads as a snowplow to clear a path in search of buried plants. A bison's fur is thick enough to keep its body warm, even when the temperature drops to forty or fifty degrees below zero Fahrenheit. That's cold but a bison's coat makes it comfortable in blizzards when other animals on the open range such as deer and antelope are in danger of freezing. Before the first snow falls, a bison already has started to grow its winter coat. Bison maintain their body heat because they are nomads, travelers on the move in search of their next meal.

Watching bison along the roadside is exciting but can be dangerous. A person who tries to get too close may find a horn in his rump. Angry cows or bulls will charge in an instant.

People who want to see bison "up close" carry binoculars or a long camera lens and use them from a safe distance. If a bison is walking along the road, it is wise to stay in the car.

31

Bison usually give warnings if people approach too closely. They might stomp a front hoof, or snort with flaring nostrils, or swirl their tails. In national parks like Yellowstone or The Badlands, people may hear bison before they see them. Bison have their own language. The bellow of a bull sounds like a roaring lion. It tells intruders or other members of the herd that he is the leader and should not be bothered. When a cow feels threatened, she often grunts. When a calf loses its mother, it starts bawling.

Bison don't have clocks, but they are most active in the mornings and evenings. When the sun gets hot, they rest to stay cool, especially during the summer. They might swim in a river or nap in the shade, but their favorite trick is to take off some "clothes." Every summer, bison shed their winter fur. They roll in the dirt or rub against a tree to work the hair loose. In the meadows, there are spots where no grass grows. These are wallows, a sure clue that you are in bison country. Wallows are formed when bison roll on the ground to scratch their backs and shake off biting flies. Dusting themselves in this dirt is a natural bug repellent.

Beneath a bison's skinny legs, rodents such as mice and kangaroo rats scramble. Under protective cover, prairie dogs and gophers search for seeds without having to worry about owls and hawks hunting them for dinner.

Bison and prairie dogs tend to live in the same places. Prairie dogs dig holes in the ground and grasses grow in the disturbed soil. Bison like that. And prairie dogs also enjoy having bison around. The bison herd stomps down the soil with their hooves which makes it easier for a prairie dog to make underground tunnels.

36

Some of the bison's best friends are cowbirds and magpies. Because there aren't many trees, birds land on the backs of bison where they can spy upon the world. This arrangement rewards both bird and beast. The bison has a friend that eats swarms of bugs off its back and the cowbird gets a free meal.

When bison can't get a cowbird to scratch an itch, they rub their woolly bodies against a lone tree or fence post.

Bison are *herbivores*, which means they eat plants. Their teeth and jaws are powerful chewing machines. Big, flat teeth called molars grind the leafy stems while sharp teeth called incisors snip plants like a scissors. To keep their faces clean, bison sometimes wipe their noses with their purple tongues. Because their bodies are so big, bison need to eat several pounds of grass or the ends of brushy twigs to give them energy every day. Unless they're resting, bison walk with their heads lowered to the ground, grazing from one patch of buffalo grass to the next.

After tugging grass from the ground, they swallow it without chewing. The grass passes down into the bison's stomach but later, when the animal is resting, the grass moves back up into a bison's mouth where it is chewed over and over again. This is a special way of removing minerals and vitamins from the food they eat. It is called "chewing cud" and sometimes a bison's jaw looks as if the animal is chomping on a big piece of bubble gum.

Once the grass is well chewed, bison swallow it for the last time. It digests in their stomachs which have four chambers—the rumen (ROO-MAN), reticulum (RAH-TICK-CUE-LUM), omasum (OH-MASS-SUM), and abomasum (AB-BOE-MASS-SUM). Then the bison leaves behind "buffalo chips," also known as dung heaps, which are dark, mushy, and flat as pancakes. Pretty soon, they bake and dry in the sun. When long-ago Native Americans and pioneers needed to make a campfire, they collected dung and burned it in place of firewood. Dung is good for the soil because it fertilizes the earth which helps plants grow. These buffalo chips have been called "decorations" of bison country. It's fun to toss them through the air like frisbees.

Sometimes, another clue on the ground shows that bison live in the area: bison tracks. The tracks are about five inches wide, and they're shaped like two lima beans facing each other.

Watching from the roadside, you might think a herd of bison is calm and fearless. But almost anything can spook a herd into stampeding across the prairie. The herd might be scared by claps of thunder, or a grassfire, or surprise invaders such as grizzly bears or people with cameras.

Bison can't see very well but they can smell and hear an enemy as it sneaks through a forest or meadow. When one bison starts to run, the entire herd may follow the leader forming a noisy, rumbling stampede. Every autumn in South Dakota, people find excitement in Custer State Park riding horses in a real bison round-up. But they must be careful to stand clear of a stampede.

For as long as anyone can remember, Indian warriors used to hunt bison on foot with bows and arrows. When Spanish explorers brought horses to the American West, chasing bison became easier. Warriers on horseback rode alongside the stampeding bison herds, driving the leader toward a cliff. These cliffs are called buffalo jumps. The animals in front ran right over the edge and tumbled hundreds of feet to their deaths.

The meat from those bison fed the entire tribe, and the hides kept people warm in winter. Nothing was wasted. The bison capes were used as warm blankets. Their hides were stretched to make tepees, moccasins and drums. And their bones became tools. To thank the bison, Native Americans offered prayers and performed special dances. In some towns, they still celebrate the bison at festivals called pow wows.

Today, some ranchers raise bison instead of cattle because bison are more gentle on the land than beef cows. When a bison eats grass, it doesn't trim the entire stalk as beef cows do, but leaves behind enough root and stem to keep the plant growing. More and more people are eating bison meat because it has less fat than beef.

Everyone who visits bison country today has a reason to celebrate. Bison are coming back and there is no longer any fear of them disappearing from the land. There are more bison alive now than there were 100 years ago—150,000 buffalo roaming across the prairies and open pastures.

Way out on the Great Plains, the earth shakes.

It's not an earthquake or growling stomachs.

Bison are home on the range.

Put your ear to the ground and listen.

The bison stampede is growing louder, and louder.